Helen Kilborn
2000

Best Of
YORK

A Unichrome Publication

Best Of YORK

CONTENTS

Introduction	6
Early York	11
York Minster	16
Walls and Bars	22
Manors and Mansions	26
York Streets	32
York All Year Round	39
Railway City	44
Journey Back in Time	46
Rivers and Bridges	48
Taking it Easy	50
Haunted York	52
City Lights	55
Beyond York	58
Index	64

Publication in this form © Pitkin Unichrome Ltd 1999
All rights reserved. No part of this publication may be reproduced, stored in a retrieval system, or transmitted, in any form or by any means, electronic, mechanical, photocopying, recording or otherwise, without prior permission of Pitkin Unichrome Ltd and the copyright holders.

Written and edited by Angela Royston
Designed by Aardvark Design Studio Ltd
Picture research by Diana Phillips
The publishers would like to thank Larch Cardoma, Blue Badge Guide for York, for reading the text

Printed in Great Britain
ISBN 1 871004 67 5 (hardback)
      1 871004 68 3 (paperback)

Acknowledgements:
Photographs are reproduced with permission of the following:
Aurora Travel Photography (Ian Booth): 12/13B;
David Birchell: 57T, 59B, 60TL;
Collections: (Ashley Cooper) 18/19B, (Michael George) 17TR, (Robert Hallmann) 17BL, (Gary Smith) 20TL, 24B, 41T, 54TR, (Liz Stares) 49B;
Alan Curtis: 9C, 12T, 21TL, 22/23B, 23B, 24TL, 25BR, 28B, 29B, 30T, 34TL&B, 35R, 37T, 39L, 42/43T, 50BL, 51T&C, 55TR, 60/61B, 62TL, 63B;

Dean & Chapter of York: inside flap, 11BL, 18BL, (Jim Kershaw) 19R, 20/21B, (Newbery Smith Photography) 20TR;
Derek Forss: 11T, 15B, 17BR, 22T, 24/25B, 27T, 28T, 32B, 40T, 44TL, 46TL;
Peter Gray: 5, 16B, 17TL, 22BL, 23TR, 31T&B, 32TL, 32/33T&B, 36TL, 36/37, 38BR, 39B, 41B, 48C, 50C, 53T, 54B, 57BR;
V.K. Guy Ltd: front cover, 2/3, 40/41B, 55B, 56T&B, 56/57B, 58B, 59C, 60B, 60/61B, 61T&B, 62TR&B, 63TL&R;
Sandra Ireland: 7B, 10T, 14/15T, 15T, 33C, 38BL, 52C, 53C;
Jorvik Viking Centre: 12/13C;
London Aerial Photo Library: 6
National Railway Museum: 44/45T&C&B;
PA Photos: 50BR;
Pitkin Unichrome: 14B, 27BL, 46TR, 53B, (Jim Kershaw) half-title, 7T, 14L, 21BR, 25T, 45CL, (Newbery) 20TR&BL, 24/25T, 26B, 30/31, 34/35T, 37B, 52/53B, (Mark Slade) 8T, 8/9B, 9T, 10B, 11BR, 18TL & TR, 19TL, 19B, 21TR, 26TL&TR, 28/29T, 29T, 35BL, 38T, 39TR, 40BL, 42T&B, 43T&B, 44TL (Peter Gray), 45CR, 48B, 48/49, 49TR, 50T, 51B, 55TL, 58TL, 58/59T, 59T, back cover (Peter Gray);
Skyscan: 16T, 22/23T, 48T;
Spectrum: 44BL, 49TL, (Keith Jones) 52T;
York Archaeological Trust: 12C, 13T&B;
York Council/Castle Museum: 12BL, 46B, 47 (all);
York Civic Trust: 30B;
York Theatre Royal: 54TL;
York Tourism Bureau: 27BR, 57BL.

INTRODUCTION

For centuries, York was the capital of the north – the second city of England. It is a medieval city built over and around a Roman one and inspired George VI to say that 'the history of York is the history of England'. The past can be seen at every turn: Danish street names evoke the thriving city of the Vikings, and medieval walls surround the Minster and much of the centre. But the city's history begins with the Romans.

The Romans

In AD71 a legion of Roman soldiers set up a military camp on the flat plain where the River Foss joined the Ouse. Having subdued the rebellious Brigantes, they built a fortress, which they called Eboracum, on the site of the present Minster. The garrison was later enlarged to hold several thousand soldiers and walls were built around it.

Little remains of the Roman garrison, or the city that grew up to service it on the south bank of the Ouse, except for the Multangular Tower, a pillar from the military headquarters and part of the Roman baths in the cellars of the Roman Bath Inn, yet the Romans remained in York for over 300 years, until around 410. They left as the Roman Empire began to collapse, and eventually were replaced by Angles from Germany who renamed the city Eoforwic.

The Angles

The Angles brought peace, learning and the return of Christianity to York. In 314, a bishop from York had been sent to the Council of Arles, but after the Romans left Christianity was probably forgotten, until Edwin, the Anglian king of Northumbria, married Ethelberga, a Christian princess from Kent. He and many of his followers were baptised in a wooden church, the forerunner of the Minster. York became a centre of learning in the 8th century and students came from all over Europe to the school of St Peter to learn from Alcuin, the great and famous scholar. Alcuin wrote a poem in which he described York as a city 'built by the Romans, high with walls and towers'.

The Vikings

In 866 Vikings from Denmark sailed up the River Ouse, captured the city and renamed it Jorvik. This was a turbulent period in England's history: one ruler quickly succeeded another, the last Danish one being Eric Bloodaxe. Yet the Vikings also traded with the local people and many converted to Christianity. Jorvik became one of the main ports in northern Europe, a centre for craftsmen and trade. The Jorvik Viking Centre is built over an excavated Viking site and recreates workshops, houses, streets and docks as they would have been. It makes use of thousands of objects found on the site.

The Normans

After the demise of Eric Bloodaxe the north was ruled by earls, under allegiance to the king. The earls, however, were rebellious and in 1066 King Harold fought and defeated them in a major battle at Stamford Bridge, close to York. Almost immediately Harold had to march south to meet the invading army of William of Normandy. Harold's exhausted army was defeated and William became king.

The northerners continued to rebel. William quashed a rebellion in York in 1068 and built a castle on the mound where Clifford's Tower now stands. When rebellion broke out again the following year, William returned to York and destroyed, not only the city, but all of the countryside between York and the River Tees, in what is called the 'Harrying of the North'. When the Domesday Book was compiled 20 years later, it recorded that 'there was not a blade of grass between the Rivers Trent and Tweed'.

Nevertheless York slowly recovered and became prosperous again. Having destroyed the wooden buildings of the Viking city, the Normans rebuilt, this time in stone. The first Norman Minster begun in 1070 was enlarged in the 12th century and later replaced by the current Minster. St Mary's Abbey and many religious houses were also built at this time.

Medieval York

By the 13th century York was again powerful. The current Minster was being built and the city walls, broken by four main bars or gates, were erected on top of the earth ramparts, constructed by the Vikings. Most of the medieval walls are still intact and provide a splendid $2\frac{1}{2}$-mile walkway around the city. York was again the capital of the north, a base from which to subdue rebellions and fight the Scots.

Kings and queens frequently visited York and, in 1298, the offices of government – the Exchequer, Chancery and Royal Law Courts – were moved here for seven years. In 1392, Richard II even considered making York the permanent capital of England. Medieval York was the second largest town in

England, with many fine buildings, churches and guildhalls. Glass for the windows was shipped up the River Ouse and painted by York's world-famous glass painters. The wool trade, and later the cloth trade, was the greatest source of wealth, but over a hundred other crafts had guilds in the city too. The most powerful was the Merchant Adventurers, the guild of overseas traders, and the Hall where they met and parts of the Guildhall survive to this day.

Each year, during the feast of Corpus Christi, the guilds performed the Mystery Plays, a cycle of 48 plays which re-enacted the stories of the Bible from the Creation to the Last Judgement. Each guild put on a play, usually one connected with their trade: the Shipwrights, for example, performed the building of the Ark and the Bakers the Last Supper. The Mystery Plays have recently been revived and are now performed every four years.

Decline and Dissolution

Even before the Tudors came to the throne, York was in decline. The wool trade decreased as York faced strong competition from London and the Hanseatic League. Hull took over as the main port for the region, and outbreaks of the plague contributed to the fall of the population.

The upheavals of the Reformation brought the destruction of many of York's beautiful religious buildings. In 1536, when Henry VIII's parliament ordered the dissolution of the smallest monasteries, Robert Aske led a rebellion, called the Pilgrimage of Grace. The rebels occupied York but were tricked into surrendering, and Robert Aske was hanged in Clifford's Tower. The dissolution of the larger monasteries followed. St Mary's Abbey and many churches were destroyed and their treasures confiscated. At the same time, however, Henry re-established the Council of the North in the King's Manor which helped York to recover economically.

Just over a hundred years later, York was again involved in conflict. The King was engaged in civil war with Parliament, and the city of York, always a royalist stronghold, was besieged by the Parliamentarians. When the city surrendered, the commander of the Parliamentarians, Lord Fairfax, ordered that 'neither churches nor other buildings shall be defaced'. It is thanks to him that so many of York's medieval treasures, particularly the magnificent stained-glass windows, were preserved for later generations.

18th-century elegance

In the 18th century trade continued to decline until York became a market town, servicing only the local area. At the same time, however, it became a social centre for the wealthy and aristocratic families of northern England. Elegant town houses and public buildings, such as the Mansion House, were built. People met in assembly rooms, in the coffee houses and at the Racecourse.

Artists and writers were drawn to York, and so were the Quakers. During the 18th century, the Quakers endowed several schools and two families started making and selling chocolate.

From the railways to the present

Three men transformed York in the 19th century. George Hudson, a self-made millionaire, brought the railways here in 1839. Within ten years, and with York at the centre, he created a rail network which covered a quarter of Britain. He became Lord Mayor of York twice and was known as the 'Railway King'. When various financial frauds came to light in 1849, Hudson's career came to an abrupt halt. York, however, continued to be an important railway city and today is visited by enthusiasts from all over the world, who come to the National Railway Museum to see the magnificent collection of railway locomotives and other fascinating items of railway history.

The chocolate companies, started in the 18th century, made good use of the railways and expanded their businesses from small shops into factories. Henry Rowntree took over the Tuke family business in 1862 and the other company became known as Terry and Sons. These names are still famous and today the companies are two of York's largest employers.

The Victorians were avid builders of civic buildings, churches, banks and schools. The City Corporation wanted to pull down the walls and bars to make way for more new buildings, but luckily a public outcry stopped them. Those same walls and bars are now a major source of income for the city, part of the historic attractions that bring thousands of tourists to York each year. Their future is secure because in 1968 the entire centre of York was made a Conservation area. Today most of the narrow streets have been pedestrianised, and the city is more vibrant and fascinating than ever.

EARLY YORK

The Multangular Tower is virtually all that remains of the Roman city walls. Built in about AD300 to strengthen the city's defences, the base of the ten-sided tower is 2 metres (6 feet) thick.

The upper stonework of the Multangular Tower is medieval, but the base, with its characteristic line of red tiles, is entirely Roman.

A solitary Roman column stands near the Minster's south entrance. It is the only survivor of 36 columns which supported a great hall, the headquarters of the Roman army, under the site of the present Minster.

When Emperor Constantius Chlorus died in York in 306, the troops proclaimed his son Constantine Emperor. He returned to Rome to fight for the title and became known as Constantine the Great. He was the first Christian Emperor of Rome, so it is doubly fitting that his statue is situated outside the Minster.

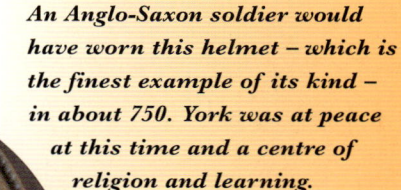

An Anglo-Saxon soldier would have worn this helmet – which is the finest example of its kind – in about 750. York was at peace at this time and a centre of religion and learning.

Every February the people of York celebrate the founding of the Viking city of Jorvik with a festival called 'Jolablot' that includes a longships regatta on the River Ouse. The Vikings sailed up the Ouse to capture York from the Saxons in 866.

The Jorvik Viking Centre is built over the excavated site of a Viking settlement. Ancient timbers from the original Viking buildings have been preserved and carefully repositioned just as they were found.

A Viking street recreated in the Jorvik Viking Centre. The street was as crowded then as it is now, though today's shoppers do not have to compete for space with flocks of geese!

Jorvik Viking Centre recreates scenes from the city in the 900s. It shows craftsmen, such as this potter at work in his pottery, using a precarious-looking system of ropes and poles to turn his wheel.

St Olave's Church, in Marygate, was founded by Siward, the Danish Earl of Northumbria, in the 11th century. Only the tower of Siward's church remains – the rest was so badly damaged during the English Civil War it had to be rebuilt.

This beautiful carved ivory horn was given to the Minster as a deed of property in about 1050. Ulf Thoroldson, the Viking ruler in Deira (West Yorkshire), decided to give his land to the Minster to prevent his two quarrelsome sons from fighting over it.

Stone arches in the Minster precincts date from the Norman period and may have formed part of a cloister in the archbishop's palace. The rest of the palace has long since disappeared, although the chapel survived and now houses the Minster Library.

Founded in 1088, St Mary's Abbey was once the most important Benedictine monastery in northern England. The elegant ruins are of the Abbey church, one of the finest religious buildings of the 13th century. After the dissolution of the Abbey, the stone was plundered to repair Beverley Minster and to build the County Gaol and the foundations of Ouse Bridge.

YORK MINSTER

York's magnificent Minster dominates the city. Its full name is the Cathedral and Metropolitical Church of St Peter in York, which means that it is the chief cathedral of the northern province of the Church of England and its patron saint is St Peter, the Apostle.

York Minster, the largest medieval Gothic church in northern Europe, took over 250 years to build, and was completed in 1472. The Minster was not the first church on this site, since Edwin, the pagan king of Northumbria, was baptised here in 627. The Minster was rebuilt several times before the current Minster was begun in 1220.

Gargoyles and beautifully intricate carvings decorate the external walls of the Minster.

The cathedral rises high above the city and can be glimpsed over the rooftops, particularly from the city walls ...

... and from nearby narrow streets.

Tall and elegant arches reach high above the nave and choir to the great east window.

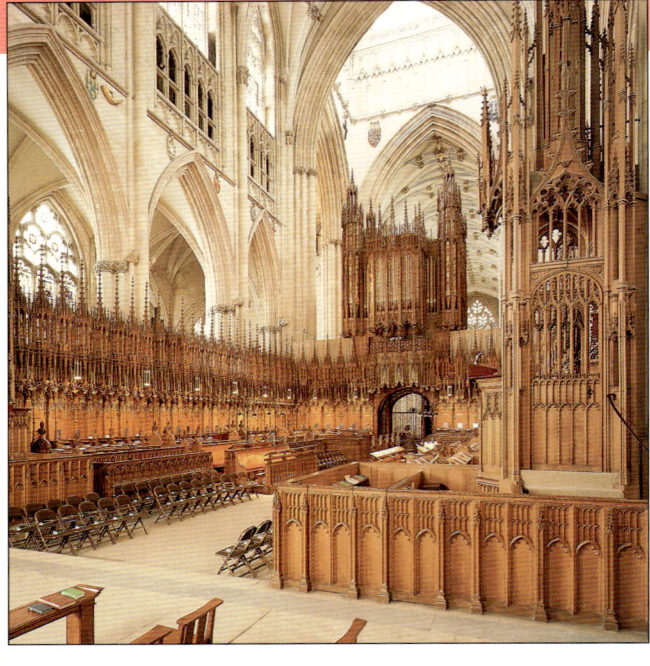

The kings of England from William 1 to Henry VI decorate the choir screen, which divides the nave and was completed in about 1461.

All the major services are sung in the choir, which, as in many cathedrals, is enclosed by screens. The choir stalls against the wall are set aside for members of the Dean and Chapter. Each has a plaque with a heraldic device associated with their office or with a church of the dioscese. The plaques also had a useful purpose – to protect the wood from the canons' hair oil.

The dragon's head which projects over the nave may have been used to raise the font cover below. A chain attached to the cover passed through a hole in the dragon's neck so that when the dragon's head was raised it lifted the cover of the font, ready for a baptism.

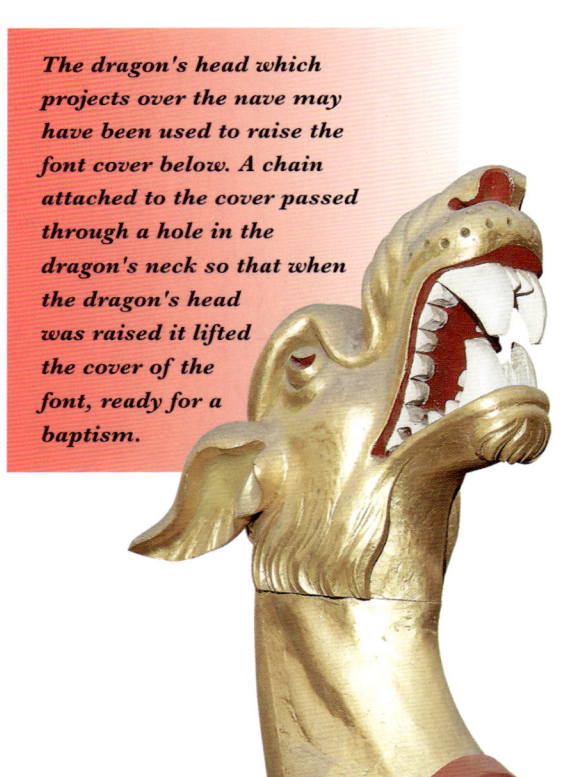

The elaborate cover of the font was designed by Sir Ninian Comper in 1947 and commemorates the baptism of King Edwin of Northumbria in 627. Since 1926 the font has been located in the crypt over what may have been a well – traditionally, but probably wrongly, supposed to be the well at which Edwin was baptised.

The carved Doomstone slab shows wicked souls being tortured in hell by devils. It was found in the garden of the Deanery and was probably part of a large scene of the Last Judgement intended to terrify church-goers in Norman times.

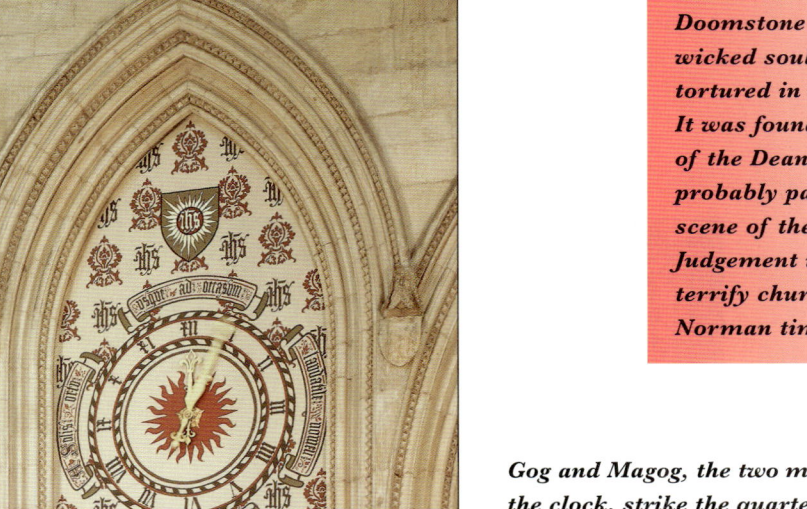

Gog and Magog, the two men-at-arms below the clock, strike the quarter hours. They were made in 1528 and are older than the current clock, which was made in 1749 by Henry Hindley, a York clockmaker. To make sure Gog and Magog do not disturb the Cathedral's worship, the striking mechanism is turned off during services.

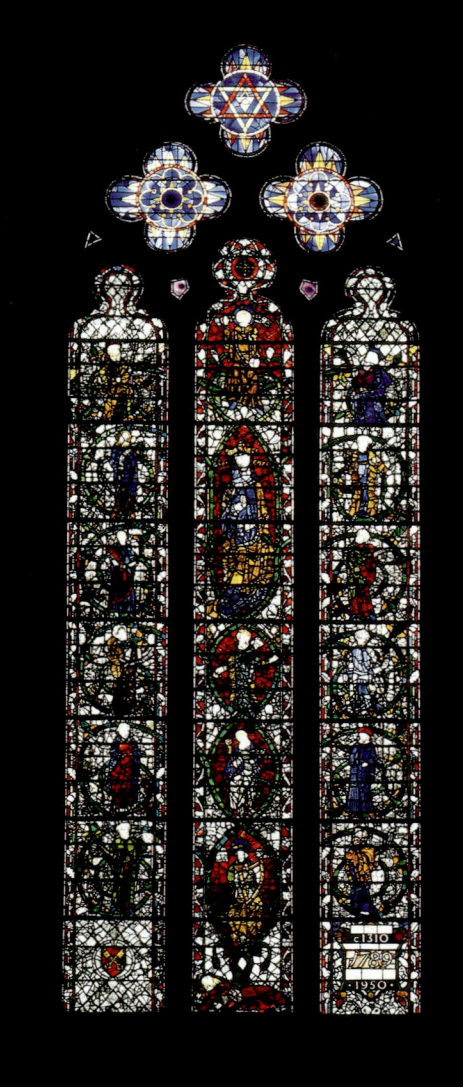

The Jesse window shows Jesus's family tree with his ancestor Jesse at the bottom and Jesus at the top.

The huge and magnificent east window is the largest area of medieval stained glass in the world. The tracery at the top shows God the Father presiding over ranks of saints and angels. The scenes beneath are from the Books of Genesis and Revelation.

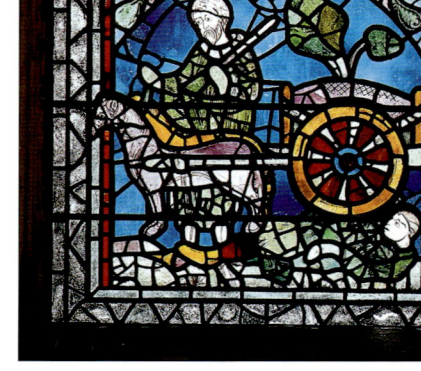

The St Nicholas stained-glass window shows the story of the Jewish money-lender who, when cheated by a Christian, called on St Nicholas to intervene. The cheat was immediately run over by a cart, which so impressed the money-lender that he converted to Christianity.

The rose window is magnificent from inside and outside. A sunflower at the centre of the stained glass is surrounded by 24 panels of white and red roses, denoting the marriage of Elizabeth of York to the Lancastrian Henry VII in 1486 which ended the Wars of the Roses.

The east end of the Minster overlooks the tranquil College Green. St William's College was built in 1461 and became home for 28 chantry priests until the Reformation.

The Minster and the pointed roof of the Chapter House rise above the Treasurer's House. The Minster is surrounded by historic buildings and beautiful gardens.

21

WALLS AND BARS

You can climb up inside Clifford's Tower and walk around the top. No one knows for sure how the Tower got its name: it may have been called after Sir Roger Clifford who was hanged here in 1322, or after the powerful Clifford family who claimed the right to be its constable.

Clifford's Tower was once the keep of York Castle and remained a garrison until the end of the 17th century. Its elegant quatrefoil walls were probably the work of Henry de Reyns, who was also involved in the building of Westminster Abbey.

In York the Danish influence means that gateways are called bars and streets are called gates. Built around an earlier Norman arch, Bootham Bar is the oldest of four main bars that allowed access into and out of the medieval city.

Walls have surrounded the city of York since Roman times, but the walls that tourists wander along today were built during the 13th and 14th centuries. Then soldiers patrolled the walls and a protective moat lapped against the outer side.

The steps lead up to the city wall at Bootham Bar.

Monk Bar shows how heavily fortified the medieval gates were. It has a heavy wooden portcullis which still works and, on top of the gate, carved men hold stones ready to drop on the enemy below.

Walmgate Bar is the only town gate in England that still has a barbican. This outer gate meant that attackers were bombarded with missiles as they tried to breach the inner gate. The stone walls bear the scars of cannon-balls and bullets from the Civil War.

The Red Tower, originally built about 1490, is the only part of the wall built of brick.

Fishergate Postern was originally built on the banks of the River Foss when the river was wider. It now stands at one end of the section of wall that stretches round to the Red Tower, on the edge of what used to be the Foss marshes.

The longest section of wall stretches around the south-west of the medieval city. Built on top of a grassy mound, the crenellated top and arrow slits are a reminder that the defence of York in medieval times was a serious business.

Micklegate Bar guarded the entrance to the city from the south. In Shakespeare's play, Henry VI, Queen Margaret orders that Richard, Duke of York's head be cut off 'and set ... on York gates, / So York may overlook the town of York'. York's head was neither the first nor the last to be displayed on Micklegate Bar.

A walk along the walls provides views and glimpses of York's historic buildings, such as this view of the Minster from Station Road.

MANORS AND MANSIONS

Built in 1361, the Merchant Adventurers' Hall is one of the best preserved medieval guildhalls in Europe. For 600 years the members controlled the trade of goods, particularly the lucrative cloth trade, into and out of the city.

The Hospitium was built in the grounds of St Mary's Abbey as a place for travellers to the Abbey to rest. The ground floor dates from around 1310, while the restored timbered first floor was added about 100 years later.

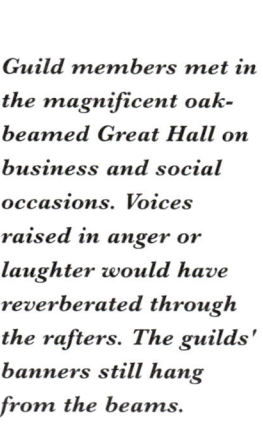

Guild members met in the magnificent oak-beamed Great Hall on business and social occasions. Voices raised in anger or laughter would have reverberated through the rafters. The guilds' banners still hang from the beams.

The medieval Guildhall built by the River Ouse in 1378 served the city's guilds. A passage runs under the Guildhall – once a medieval alleyway called Commonhall Lane.

In 1942 an air raid destroyed much of the Guildhall. The present hall is an exact reconstruction, each oak pillar being cut from a single tree trunk. The Inner Chamber, with its panelled walls with secret doors and stairways, survived the raid.

Barley Hall is a reconstruction of the medieval hospice which stood here in the 1480s. It belonged to Nostell Priory and was used as a kind of hotel, a place for visiting clerics and others to stay. Coffee Yard now runs right through part of the 15th-century building, between the great hall on one side and the kitchens (now gone), buttery and pantry on the other side.

27

Overshadowed by York Minster's splendid east end, St William's College became home for the chantry priests at about the time that the building of the Minster was completed. After the Reformation it passed into private ownership, and, when Charles I moved his court to York in 1642, it was used to house the royal printing press.

The Warden's House, attached to the King's Manor. The estate has long played a part in York's history. Originally built in 1270 as the Abbot's House for St Mary's Abbey, it was rebuilt after the Dissolution of the Monasteries. Henry VIII, James I and Charles I all stayed here, and during the Civil War it was attacked and damaged by Cromwell's troops.

Until the Reformation the Treasurer's House was the home of the Treasurer, the man in charge of the finances and treasures of the Minster. The present confusion of architecture was mainly introduced in 1897 when Frank Green bought the house and renovated it according to his own ideas and taste.

King's Manor has been altered and extended many times. After the Civil War it was used for a variety of purposes including, in Victorian times, a school for the blind. It was restored in 1964 and is now part of York University.

Ten years after the Red House was built in 1714 by Sir William Robinson, the then Lord Mayor, the city wanted it to become the mayor's official residence. Sir William would have none of it, however, so a new Mansion House was built the following year.

29

The grand and elegant Mansion House, built between 1725 and 1730, was designed to reflect York's position as the social centre of northern England. It is not usually open to the public because the Lord Mayor still lives here.

The dining room of Fairfax House, with the table laid for dinner in Georgian style. In the 1750s architect John Carr created Fairfax House, one of the finest Georgian houses in York, for the 9th Viscount of Fairfax. The house later fell on hard times and was used as a club and dance hall before being restored.

The Assembly Rooms were opened in 1732 as a place where fashionable men and women could meet, play cards and 'be seen'. At that time lords and ladies from all over England came to York for the August races. The Rooms were restored to their former splendour in 1990 and include a restaurant and tearoom.

Pictures in York City Art Gallery span over 600 years of painting and cover most countries in western Europe. One collection records the changing city as seen through the eyes of artists from 1678 to the 20th century.

The elegant De Grey Rooms in St Leonard's Place were built by G.T. Andrews as an officers' mess in 1841 and were used for concerts and public meetings.

YORK STREETS

For 900 years the Shambles was a street of butchers and slaughterhouses. The meat was displayed on the shelves in front of the open windows and, without refrigerators, the smell must have been overwhelming. A hundred years ago there were still 31 butchers in the Shambles, but today only one remains, in Little Shambles.

Narrow, winding streets, criss-crossed by alleyways, fill the area between the Minster and Clifford's Tower. The Shambles, one of the best preserved medieval streets in Europe, has buildings that date back to 1350.

Whip-Ma-Whop-Ma-Gate, the shortest street in York, is scarcely longer than its name. It is squeezed between Pavement and The Stonebow.

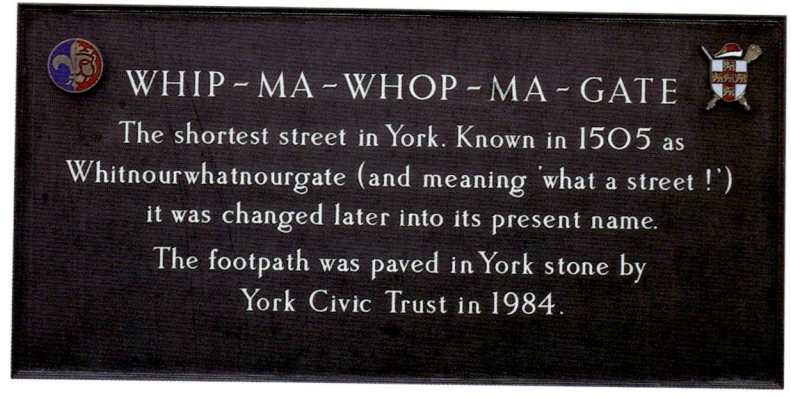

WHIP-MA-WHOP-MA-GATE
The shortest street in York. Known in 1505 as Whitnourwhatnourgate (and meaning 'what a street!') it was changed later into its present name.
The footpath was paved in York stone by York Civic Trust in 1984.

St Helen's Square is the centre of modern York. The square was created in 1745 out of the graveyard of St Helen's churchyard. The church itself was threatened with destruction several times, but has survived and is now the Civic Church.

Many shops, pubs and coffee houses have evocative signs.

The narrow street of High Petergate runs into Low Petergate and together they follow the route of Via Principalis, one of two main roads that crossed the Roman garrison.

Stonegate embodies much of the history of York. It follows the route of the Roman road, Via Praetoria, but gets its name 'gate' from the Vikings and is one of the finest medieval streets in England. Ye Olde Starre Inne is thought to be the oldest ale house in York.

This little devil squats under the eaves of No. 33 Stonegate. He is not there for any evil purpose, but to show that the building was once a printer's. Printer's devils were errand-boys whose job included carrying hot metal type.

Some of Stonegate's buildings have particular claims to fame. The half-timbered Mulberry Hall has been standing in Stonegate since 1434, before the building of the Minster itself was finally completed.

In the 19th century this medieval house in Stonegate was given a new frontage of Minton tiles. The two styles blend together to make a beautiful façade.

The great clock outside St Martin-le-Grand in Coney Street has the face of Father Time on the side and a figure known as the Little Admiral on top. The admiral is using a cross staff, an early kind of sextant, to find the altitude of the Sun and so calculate his position of latitude.

35

A golden sheep hangs above the Golden Fleece next to the half-timbered Herbert House in Pavement. The house dates from 1557 and belonged to Sir Thomas Herbert, a friend of Charles I. Sir Thomas kept Charles company during the night before his execution and walked with him to the scaffold. In return, Charles gave Sir Thomas his watch.

Alleys in York are often called 'snickelways'. Ogleforth is a narrow alley that leads from Goodramgate into the cobbled Chapter House Street.

There is plenty of space in Parliament Street to sit down and catch your breath – before resuming the serious business of shopping.

Lady Row cottages in Goodramgate are 14th-century and form the oldest row of houses in York. About 100 years ago, archaeologists found many Viking artifacts in Goodramgate, giving weight to the theory that the street was named after Gutherum, a Viking chieftain.

As the musician plucks the strings and taps his foot, the puppet dances. You never know what you will see next ...

... portrait painting, for example...

... or mime, on the streets of York.

YORK ALL YEAR ROUND

A walk along the city wall can be cold and windy, but in spring hundreds of daffodils on the outer bank and on the mound around Clifford's Tower promise warmth to come.

Spring blossom on Queen's Walk outside the Minster. The brightly painted house is part of the Minster choir school.

In summer hanging flower baskets add a cascade of colour to the City War Memorial gardens by the River Ouse.

Boxes of geraniums and Sweet William line the Shambles and provide some shade for the people below.

Summer flowers brighten the garden beneath the city wall on Station Road.

Pigeons look for seeds in Museum Gardens, as the leaves begin to turn autumnal.

Washed clean after a shower of rain, the pavement along College Street gleams with reflections.

41

Every Christmas a fair with a helter-skelter and roundabouts is held in Parliament Street.

Christmas lights add to the pleasure of shopping in York. As a cold December day draws to a close, bright lights bring out the warmth and friendliness of York's shopkeepers.

Clear blue skies and a thin carpet of snow add to the elegance of St Mary's Abbey.

York Minster stands solid against the cold winter weather. The Minster has survived much in its 800-year history, including cracks in the walls and three major fires.

In winter, the shady tranquillity of College Green is replaced by bright skies and long shadows. The winter sun never rises high above the roof-tops.

RAILWAY CITY

The National Railway Museum is the largest and finest railway museum in the world. It charts the history of the railways from Stephenson's Rocket to the Channel Tunnel. This photo, taken on a 360 degree camera, shows an all-round view of the locomotives in the Great Hall.

Visitors can climb into historic locomotives from the North Eastern Railway Company ...

The first train steamed into York in 1839 and transformed travel to and from the city. When Thomas Prosser's magnificent railway station was built in 1877 it was the largest in Europe. Today's rail travellers still marvel at the huge curved roof, with its cast-iron rafters supported on slender Corinthian columns.

The locomotive Rocket, built by George Stephenson, triumphed in the Rainhill Trials in 1829, so persuading people to use steam trains on the new public railway between Liverpool and Manchester.

In 1852 all station clocks and guards' watches were set to Greenwich Mean Time and the effort to make trains run on time began.

...or into Mallard, *the fastest steam engine ever.*

Another all-round view of the Museum. It shows porters' trolleys, carriages and other railway equipment.

45

JOURNEY BACK IN TIME

When you walk along Kirkgate in the Castle Museum you are back in Victorian times. The street has been meticulously recreated just as it was, with cobblestones, shop fronts and hansom cab.

The Castle Museum is housed in the former female and debtors' prisons. It was started by Dr John Kirk, a country doctor from Pickering who, in the first half of the 20th century, collected traditional everyday items that were no longer used. The Museum is now the most popular folk museum in the country.

A reconstruction of the main room in a moorland cottage. The portrait of the young Queen Victoria shows that it comes from the middle of the 19th century. The room includes a bed and crib as well as the kitchen stove and spinning wheel.

This fan and the beautiful items of jewellery would have belonged to a wealthy Yorkshire woman in the 19th century.

The Gypsy Caravan was built in 1897 by Billy Wright of Rothwell Haigh, near Leeds. The inside is stained red in the traditional manner. The outside was repainted in 1962 by Jimmy Berry, the last survivor of caravan painters.

This Edwardian hardware shop has been recreated in Half Moon Court in the Castle Museum. In this shop it was possible to buy a whole range of everyday items, from carpet beaters to keys and balls of string.

47

RIVERS AND BRIDGES

Several bridges cross the River Ouse. In the foreground is Ouse Bridge with Lendal Bridge and Scarborough Bridge, the railway bridge, further up river. The Ouse flows into the Humber Estuary and the North Sea.

King's Staith was once a busy working quay. From Roman times until the arrival of the railways, York's trade was carried up and down the river by barge and boat.

Today people still travel the rivers on pleasure boats, rowing boats and barges, while others enjoy walking along the riverbanks.

48

The rectangular Lendal Tower stands at one end of Lendal Bridge and…

… the circular Barker Tower stands at the other end. In medieval times before the bridge was built, if York was threatened with invasion, a chain was stretched between the two towers to stop enemy ships sailing into the city.

Skeldergate Bridge was built of iron and stone in 1881. At that time, part of the bridge could be raised to allow sailing ships to pass through to the staithes.

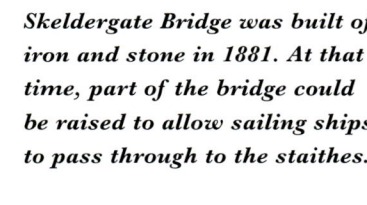

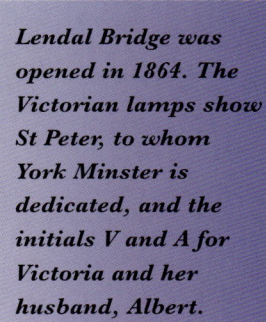

Lendal Bridge was opened in 1864. The Victorian lamps show St Peter, to whom York Minster is dedicated, and the initials V and A for Victoria and her husband, Albert.

TAKING IT EASY

The streets of York are densely packed, but there are plenty of beautiful gardens, open green spaces and places to relax. Dean's Park offers a tranquil view of the Minster.

Stop for a while and watch one of York's street performers. Wait to see what he does next.

Even in the busy streets there are places to relax, talk to friends and have a cup of tea.

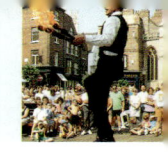

For those who have had enough of sight-seeing, there is plenty of space by the river just to sit and dangle their legs.

The open-topped tour bus gives a fine view, with an interesting commentary, of Clifford's Tower and many other city sights.

York's famous racecourse provides an exciting day out. The most famous races are the Ebor Festival, held in August.

A boat ride on the river is one of the most relaxing ways to see the medieval Guildhall and catch some unusual views of the city.

HAUNTED YORK

York's most ancient ghosts are a company of Roman foot soldiers who appeared through the wall of the cellars of the Treasurer's House. They were first seen in 1953 when they terrified a young plumber working there. It is now known that the Treasurer's House was built over a Roman road.

Listen out for ghostly footsteps if you enter St William's College. They are said to belong to one of two brothers who murdered a clergyman over 400 years ago. Overwhelmed by guilt, the younger brother hung himself and the elder brother paced the corridors and rooms.

King's Manor claims two ghosts – a monk and a Tudor woman dressed in green and, perhaps disappointed in love, clutching a bunch of roses.

In 1586 Margaret Clitheroe, a Roman Catholic, was caught sheltering priests from persecution and punished by being crushed to death with weights placed on a large door over her body. Her shrine is in the busy, noisy Shambles but it emanates an uncanny sense of peace.

Many mourners have seen a mysterious and beautiful woman at the entrance to All Saints' Church in Pavement. She has long hair and a shimmering white dress and she appears only at funeral processions. She beckons the procession into the church and then disappears.

The church of St Mary in Bishophill claims an unusual ghost, particularly for a church. The sound of coins are heard sliding, one by one, across an invisible table before falling into a metal box. When the last coin has slid in, the lid is slammed shut with a startlingly loud bang.

53

The actors in the Theatre Royal never know when there might be an extra, ghostly member of the audience. The Grey Lady only appears occasionally, but, when she does, the production is always a success.

In 1572 Thomas Percy, Earl of Northumberland, was executed in Pavement and his head displayed on Micklegate Bar until it was buried in Holy Trinity churchyard in 1574. It is said that a headless ghost has been seen in the churchyard, supposedly Thomas Percy searching for his lost head.

The Black Swan pub in Peasholme Green has more than one ghost. Sometimes a beautiful woman is seen gazing into the fire. At other times a man in a bowler hat seems to be waiting irritably for someone to come, but after a while gives up and slowly fades away.

CITY LIGHTS

Lights and floodlights highlight the drama of York's magnificent buildings and views. The Minster, bathed in light, rises above the rooftops, and the camera captures a ghostly, colourful trail of passing head-lamps and tail lights.

The monument on College Green is silhouetted against the floodlit east end of the Minster.

Green floodlights illuminate Clifford's Tower, high on its mound overlooking the Castle Museum.

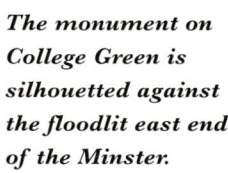

Night adds mysterious charm to the Shambles and alleyways.

The Mansion House looks even more imposing at night than it does during the day.

Bright lights in Stonegate make shopping a pleasure even after dark.

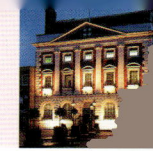

Illuminations along the riverside throw reflections on the water, creating a romantic setting for an evening walk.

The arched window gives an inviting glimpse of the inside of Little Betty's in Stonegate.

A torchlight procession lights up the streets of York during the Viking festival.

BEYOND YORK

York is at the centre of a beautiful area of Britain. The Yorkshire Dales, North York Moors and coast are a few hours' drive away, and even closer are many famous country houses, abbeys and villages.

The tall bridge in Knaresborough carries the railway line across the River Nidd. Below is Mother Shipton's Cave – a small, dark grotto, called after a supposed witch in the 16th century.

Beningbrough Hall is a Georgian country house, built by William Thornton for John Bourchier in 1716. Inside are an exquisitely carved staircase and rooms furnished with many 18th-century pieces. There is a display of paintings by Reynolds, Gainsborough and other 18th-century artists, on loan from the National Portrait Gallery.

Harewood House is a stately home on a grand scale. It was designed by John Carr and built of stone quarried on the estate. Inside, the largest collection of Chippendale furniture is lavishly shown in the rooms designed by Robert Adam. Outside, a vast parkland, laid out by Capability Brown, includes a bird garden where birds are bred in captivity.

Cow and Calf Rocks overlook the famous Ilkley Moor.

The ruins of Fountains Abbey give an idea of the magnificence of the Abbey before it was destroyed and its treasures stolen by Henry VIII's men. The original abbey was founded by a group of monks who left St Mary's Abbey in York in 1132 to establish a new abbey by the River Skell.

The ruins of Bolton Abbey have been a source of inspiration for poets and artists, including Wordsworth and Turner.

The spectacular Aysgarth Falls on the River Ure near Wensleydale.

The huge bulk of 'Fat Betty', a medieval cross, stands out on the wild bleak North York Moors, near Rosedale.

Villages, like Muker in Swaledale, nestle among the rolling hills of the Dales. Sheep graze in some fields while buttercups run riot in others.

Helmsley Castle was built by one of the knights of William the Conqueror. During the English Civil War the Parliamentarians laid siege to the castle for three months, leaving it in ruins.

Malham Cove provides a wonderful backdrop for walkers and hikers.

Rievaulx Abbey was the first Cistercian monastery to be founded in the north of England. Even before the Dissolution of the Monasteries, the monastery had become too big and parts had been pulled down. The surviving tiers of arches show the Abbey's original height and grandeur.

A narrow beck, or stream, winds through the small town of Helmsley, evoking an idyllic past.

Castle Howard is one of the country's greatest houses. It was built by Charles Howard, third Earl of Carlisle, in 1699 to replace his castle which had been destroyed by fire. He employed the playwright Sir John Vanbrugh as the architect, an inspired choice who produced a building of dramatic proportions.

Whitby Abbey, on the cliff above the town, overlooks the narrow, cobbled streets and harbour below.

Burton Agnes Hall near Bridlington is an imposing Jacobean manor.

Scarborough is a popular resort on the east coast of Yorkshire.

63

INDEX

All Saints' church 53
Angles 6–7, 12
Anglo-Saxon see Angles
Aske, Robert 9
Assembly Rooms 30
Aysgarth Falls 60

Barley Hall 27
Beningbrough Hall 59
Black Swan 54
Bolton Abbey 60
Bootham Bar 22, 23
Burton Agnes Hall 63

Castle Howard 62
Castle Museum 46–47, 55
Clifford's Tower 9, 22, 39, 55
Civil War 9, 14, 28, 61
Chocolate companies 10
Constantine, Emperor 12

De Grey Rooms 31

Edwin, king of Northumbria 7

Fairfax, Lord 9
Fairfax House 30
Fishergate Postern 24
Fountains Abbey 59

Gardens 40, 41, 50
Ghosts 52–54
Goodramgate 37
Guildhall 9, 27, 51

Harewood House 59
Helmsley Castle 61

Helmsley 62
Holy Trinity 54
Hospitium 26
Hudson, George 10

Jorvik Viking Centre 13, 14

King's Manor 28, 52
King's Staith 48
Knaresborough 58

Lendal Bridge 48, 49

Mansion House 10, 30, 56
Minster 8, 16–21, 25, 39, 43, 50, 55
Multangular Tower 6, 11
Medieval York 8–9, 16–21, 22–25, 26–28, 32, 34, 37
Merchant Adventurers' Hall 9, 26
Micklegate Bar 25
Monk Bar 23
Mystery plays 9

National Railway Museum 44–45
Normans 7–8, 15

Ogleforth 36

Parliament Street 37, 42, 50
Pavement 36
Petergate 33

Quakers 10

Railways 10
Red House 29

Red Tower 24
Reformation 9, 28, 29
Richard II 8
Rievaulx Abbey 62
Romans 6, 11, 12, 33, 34, 52

St Helen's Square 33, 50
St Martin-le-Grand 35
St Mary's Abbey 8, 9, 15, 26, 28, 42, 59
St Mary of Bishophill 53
St Olave's Church, Marygate 14
St William's College 21, 28, 52
Scarborough 63
Shambles 32, 40, 53, 56
Skeldergate Bridge 49
Stained glass 9, 20, 21
Stonegate 34–35, 56
Swaledale 60

Theatre Royal 54
Treasurer's House 21, 29, 52

Vikings 7, 13, 14, 34, 37
Viking Festival 13, 57

Walls 8, 22–25, 39, 40, 55
Walmgate Bar 24
Whip-Ma-Whop-Ma-Gate 32
Whitby 63
William of Normandy 7

York City Art Gallery 31